Just Us Girls at Work ™

To

_____

From

_____

Just Us Girls at Work ™

Copyright ©1999 FrontPorch Books,
a division of Garborg's LLC

Written by Julie Sutton
Illustrated by Angela Jarecki

Design by Lecy Design

Published by Garborg's LLC
P. O. Box 20132, Bloomington, MN 55420

Scripture quotations marked TLB are taken from the Living Bible © 1971.
Used by permission of Tyndale House Publishers, Inc., Wheaton, Illinois 60189.
All rights reserved.

Scripture quotations marked NIV are taken from the Holy Bible, New International Version®.
Copyright © 1973, 1978, 1984 by International Bible Society.
Used by permission of Zondervan Publishing House.

ISBN 1-58375-473-3
Printed in Mexico

Just Us Girls™ at Work

Just Us Girls™

Written by Julie Sutton

Illustrated by Angela Jarecki

FrontPorch
BOOKS

Dedication:

Dedicated to busy women everywhere who somehow manage to get it all done—on their lunch hour!

To enjoy your work and accept your lot in life—that is indeed a gift from God.

ECCLESIASTES 5:19 TLB

Introduction:

As more and more of us try on new styles of making a living—part-timers, telecommuters, freelancers like ourselves—the working woman of today has many faces. In Just Us Girls™ at Work we offer a few humble observations that we hope will put a smile on yours.

Having spent many years of our lives in various working environments, from factories to corporate cubicles to our own noisy home offices, we have discovered three essentials to survival on the job: 1) a good friend, 2) a good sense of humor, and 3) a good deal of prayer.

Above all, we've discovered there's nothing so gratifying as doing what you enjoy and being paid for it. Our prayer is that you will find this to be your experience, as it is ours.

Enjoy.

Julie and Angela,
creators of Just Us Girls™

I need someone like you at the office.
Not only as great moral support...but
as a safeguard against leaving the
women's restroom with my skirt
tucked into my pantyhose!

Ladies and gentlemen!
Introducing this year's winner and
still champion at "Getting Things
Done on Her Lunch Hour!"

Remember when the only virus warnings you got were from your mother?

Raises, bonuses, benefits, promotions...these are the minor compensations for all of our hard work. Friendships like ours—now, these are the REAL career rewards!

Rumor has it there's an opening for Nicest Person on the Planet...but I'm afraid you're overqualified.

"I love doing lunch with you. It's such a proactive way to leverage our synergy in a win-win relationship."

Friends don't let friends talk like this.

It ought to be a rule of thumb that at the end of the day, a woman deserves to be held for the same amount of time she has spent on hold.

Call screening:
My friends know I'm home but if I answer the phone, how can I get my work done?

Call waiting:
I hate to ask someone to hold so I can take another call, but it might be important business.

Caller ID:
Is it okay to call a number back even if no message was left, just in case it was urgent?

Remember when the only socially unacceptable telephone behavior was listening in on a party line?

Disposing of sensitive documents is no problem for me. My home office is equipped with a handy-dandy paper shredder!

Office Etiquette

TIP NUMBER 497:

Once you've actually arrived at the office, it is generally frowned upon to continue hitting the "snooze" button.

Who needs lengthy analysis of annual report figures and financial spreadsheets? I figure we could easily increase our BOTTOM LINE with longer coffee breaks and an extra slice of cheesecake!

How to tell if you're overworked:

✓ Management's idea of "flex time" is letting you lift weights on your lunch hour.

✓ Your mind doesn't operate in "brainstorm mode" anymore. It's more like a low-lying cloud cover.

✓ You've considered job sharing, but can't find the necessary eight willing partners to divide the tasks.

Louise's entire department misunderstood management's directive regarding "budget cuts."

Re-entering the work force after years of parenting can be a little intimidating. "The nurture, education and preparation of young human beings for full, productive lives in the twenty-first century" means a lot to me, but how will it look on a résumé?

You will be blessed when you come in and blessed when you go out.

DEUTERONOMY 28:6 NIV

In the workplace it's very important to me that I have visibility with essential contacts. I look awful in glasses.

Full Timers, Part Timers, Temps,
Free Lancers, Consultants, Home Business
Owners, Home Schoolers...there's just one
title for women that has become
obsolete: "Lady of Leisure!"

Singing for Dummies
Electricity for Dummies
Shoelace tying for Dummies
Planting for Dummies
Parking for Dummies
Drawing for Dummies
Gardening for Dummies
Snorkling for Dummies
Pencil Sharpening for Dummies
Dishwashing for Dummies
Quantum Physics for Dummies
Eating for Dummies
Typing for Dummies
Flying for Dummies
Working for Dummies
Shopping for Dummies
Mowing for Dummies
Meetings for Dummies
Brain Surgery for Dummies
Physics for Dummies
Cooking for Dummies
Modems for Dummies
Driving for Dummies
Exercise for Dummies

Boy, these "For Dummies" books really run the gamut!

On my way to work I pray my tires won't have a blow-out because I'm not carrying a spare...during the day I pray the same thing for my pantyhose!

You know you're really stressed when you start having more breakdowns than the office copier.

My husband says there's a computer virus out there called the "Lady Bug." It doesn't destroy any of your files; it just cleans up your desktop so you can't find anything.

"No, you didn't interrupt my work.
I'm just trying to determine which of
my 'In Baskets' holds the most pressing
items at the moment."

These days everyone is hiring outside consultants to tell them how to run things. Why couldn't this work for personal relationships?

"Don't date him. He'll never commit."
"Your family interferes too much."
"screen your calls."
"Buy the higher price cat food."

Sometimes in the middle of the work day, I stop, look around me and wonder aloud, "Is this all there is?" Then someone plops more papers in my In Box and says, "Nope—there's more where this came from!"

A certain circular reasoning applies to work. It's often while you're jumping through hoops that you feel most left out of the loop.

Lord, help me to get along with
the difficult people in my life. Especially
those who are probably praying this
prayer about me right now....

There Ought to Be a Law

"Oh, sorry. I forgot to tell you, I have you on speaker phone. Now, what were you saying about your unwanted facial hair?"

Office Etiquette

TIP #112:

Regardless of how good-
looking Jack in Accounting is,
it is considered unprofessional
to close an inter-office memo
with "Luv 'n Kisses—Here's my home phone number!"

To Jack: Acct. Dept

Here's my home
phone number
555--5683

Sigh...I can remember when "massive reorganization"
meant color-coding my closets and "downsizing" was
the result of a successful diet!

Heaven help us.
Corporate-speak is everywhere.

"This value-adding hairstyle will
definitely differentiate you in
the workplace and ensure your
competitive advantage."

Electronic organizers are replacing bulky planners;
we talk on lightweight cell phones and carry around
laptop computers.... If technology is so adept at
dropping excess poundage, when are they going
to do something about my hips?!

Success means different things to different people.

If I manage to coordinate schedules with my family
members and have a real sit-down dinner a couple
times a week, I consider myself a "major player."

I attend corporate seminars so I can add to my skill set and maximize my potential in order to enhance my professional success and personal productivity. Plus, there's usually free food.

During particularly boring meetings, I like to play "Fishing for My Pumps Underneath the Conference Table While Appearing Alert and Interested."

Little did we know as young children how valuable those playground skills would become.

"Phone tag! You're It!"

Never underestimate the value of a praying friend. The outcome of many a crucial meeting has been determined by a 5-second phone prayer!

The world will never be a
perfect place until someone invents
a purse that's both organizationally
sound and user-friendly.

Interoffice mail is too slow. E-mail is too impersonal. Voice mail is too one-sided. Will we ever give up that age-old quest for the perfect mail?

Work smarter, not harder—that's my motto!
Unfortunately, my In Box doesn't appear to share
my business philosophies....

On those tough days, having you for a friend is such
a godsend.... It's like arriving ten minutes late but
finding a parking space close to the elevator.

I don't know about "swimming with the sharks"—most days it feels more like "grumbling with the guppies."

Office Etiquette

TIP NUMBER 223:

If you're bored in the middle of the afternoon and want company, employing the positive olfactory properties of microwave popcorn is considered an acceptable maneuver.

The female of the species is uniquely gifted by her Creator. She can bear and raise children...conduct business dealings shrewdly and profitably...and flawlessly apply lipliner at speeds exceeding 60 mph.

At the end of a rough day, remember: God created cheesecake for such a time as this. After all, it's no coincidence that "stressed" spelled backwards is "desserts"!

Footwear

Irony at its height:

the clothing of choice for women who represent the well-educated, high-achiever bracket...

- dangerously unstable, uncomfortable footwea

- thin, flimsy leg coverings that last about a day—if you're extremely careful

- restrictive jacket and skirt constructed of unyielding fabric requiring expensive dry cleaning

Mandatory overtime is when I have to cancel a ski trip to work over the weekend. Voluntary overtime is when I stay late at the office to get out of cleaning my oven.

Since the 1980s I've gone from an optimist to a pessimist to a realist...now I'm just like everyone else—a survivalist!

My times are in your hands.

PSALM 31:15 TLB

TGIF!

(Thank God for Invaluable friendships!)
Your net worth is off the charts!